AF244184

Contents

Introduction

Flowing Thoughts is a journey through the overthinking, complex mind of a teenager. Each poem narrates its own unique story, which will be viewed differently by every reader, whether adult or teenager. This collection offers an insight into my mind: a struggling teenage boy trying to discover his place in the world before he leaves home to start a new life—under his own rule, under his own roof, under his own order.

From this, the thoughts that inspire each of these poems have been plucked from my stress-filled and pressurised mind. Questions such as, "What will I miss?", "Who will I miss?", and "What is before me?" provided the tools I needed to create deeply personal and emotive poetry.

Each poem in *Flowing Thoughts* carries its own personal meaning, inspired by the experiences and epiphanies I've had over the past year—through the people I've met, the moments I've shared, and the emotions I've felt. However, I believe what I've written isn't just for me, nor for those who've inspired me, nor for those who might know the true meaning behind the text. In fact, it's for everyone. Teenagers might relate to the language, finding similarities in their own often-confused lives. Adults might look back on their teenage years and discover a connection between what they felt and what I feel. There's no target reader for this collection; no reserved seat in the theatre of my mind. It's free entry, with no limits and no discrimination.

The themes in each poem are universally relatable. Every human being has experienced the emotions detailed in this collection's various poems. If not, they'll find a connection to their own personal life through each one and the matters they discuss. The themes these poems contain are intentionally chosen to resonate deeply with the reader.

These themes include:

Love
Loss
Future
Doubt
Regret
Insecurities
Joy
Hate
Belief

All the themes chosen within this collection are meant to reflect the flowing thoughts of a teenager. The themes listed above all interlock, with the true essence of each poem remaining unclear and uncertain, much like the life of a teenager.

My life isn't special. I'm a seventeen-year-old boy from Belfast, Northern Ireland. I go to school, I have friends both in and outside of it, I like football, and I listen to music. I have passions and aspirations I work towards. I'm in love with a girl who will never see me the way I see her. I've navigated my share of ups and downs but always find a way through. I have a loving family, and I love them. I'm just a teenager.

I'm glad I wasn't born into an unnatural world; I'm glad I can narrate how I feel in writing, so perhaps someone who reads this won't feel alone in their experiences. If they do feel alone and happen to read this, know that everything will be okay. It will all work out when we're older, I promise.

Life is complex; we learn that from day one. The moment we open our eyes and see the many doctors surrounding us at birth, or when we look at our mother for the first time and know this will be a love that will never die—these initial experiences introduce us to life's intricate nature. These complexities will continue until the day we close our eyes for the last time and go to rest, knowing there will be even more complexities after we are gone. I wanted to share some of the complexities I felt during my teenage years, spanning from when I started considering my future until I was just months away from writing the next chapter in my life.

I hope to inspire others to share their own flowing thoughts of confusion and complexity, no matter what form that may take. If they can vocalise it, that's what truly matters to me.

-Cairnsy

Content

For Tom,

Your bravery and confidence have convinced me to write this collection.

You are an inspiration.

You are a good man. You are incredible.

I love you bro.

First published in 2024
By TM Publishings.

Printed in the United Kingdom.
All Rights Reserved.
© TM Publishings, 2025

All poems originally written and owned by:
Jack Cairns

Tom Moore
TMPublishings
www.tmpublishings.com

ISBN 978-1-0682436-1-5

Jack Cairns'

Flowing Thoughts

The confusing and conflicting thoughts of a teenager.

Life of Lives

A day of days, a month of months, a life of lives,
That was the atmosphere which surrounded my being.
The air I suck deep into my lungs is sweet,
Like a zest to compliment a perfect meal,

And my starters were something I've had each morning,
Each afternoon and each evening. My delightful family.
The first and most important feast in this restaurant,
The one to set the standard for the quality of all else in this
life.

My main is all I've ever known, all who've shown me love
and care.
Those who I have seen every day and not changed,
Being truthful and being real. Simply inspiring.
A group so comfortable in their own skin. A group I am
proud to be in.

And, of course, my dessert is you.
The sweetheart of my life, with a coating of perfection,
And the one part of my meal I shall *never* turn down.
The cherry on top to the life of lives.

Immortal

I used to live my life in fear, mainly a fear of "After."
Questions filled my life in every moment of doubt
Of what will become of me. But I continue to ask myself:
"What will become of me?"
What exactly is my purpose on this land?
I am aware I have people who really care,
Possibly even love me. So, my thoughts are not negative,
Just consumed by an ardent curiosity of what happens after,
And if my life was of huge significance to the world.
These thoughts will continue for years to come,
And won't stop after I excel into stardom.
That ardent curiosity will continue.
The curiosity of the Unknown.
"Is there God?" I'd like to believe there is,
Despite him placing me into confusion.
Yet I love him ever so.
Or maybe there is only Satan? But not with big red horns
Who guides me down into the fiery pit of Pandemonia,
But just a man who was once placed into confusion
But he escaped quicker than all else.
Yet I do not sympathize with him, for I know my way.
And still, despite my guidance, I *still* ask myself,
"What comes next? Why do I fear it?
Have I done enough to fulfil the plan?"

But, in that moment I realized something that must be
shared.
An epiphany that all humans shall encounter.
That one day, each man's heart will beat its final beat,
Their lungs will breathe their final breath.
But it's what that man does for others in his life makes him,
Immortal.

Singing Trees

I passed a garden for the Queen, long gone,
And my ears enlightened to the trees singing sweet songs.
In song, they bounce, and they pounce on every note,
The illusion is made they are alive, not remote.

Singing songs of imagination and dreams,
Fooling its listeners to believe not as it seems.
With a lime-green look and tall, gaunt figure,
To the poor, joy radiates bigger and bigger!

A fantastical illusion made of mechanics and robots,
A chance for laughs in our life must not be forgot.
How something so small can make joy have such a sound,
It gives me hope that true happiness can be found.

No ecstasy to remove us from reality needed,
As a singing tree helped discover where happiness is seeded.
I wish we all had a singing tree in our lives,
To help us all discover where true happiness thrives.

My Christine,

My Christine,

I have no more words, for once I am totally silent.
Silent because I have said all I must.
The day we met will remain one I will keep dear to my
heart for my life,
Your bright smile, your glowing eyes, your hair always
perfect—you.
You were perfect; even if you could not see it, you were
perfect for me.
And yes, we were in love, we both knew it for certain, we
were in love.
Yet I ignored it; my selfish desires overcame me, and I lost
you.
I do not know what overcame me that day I confessed to
you,
What I have been trying to say finally escaped the cage of
secrecy,
but it needed to be said.
You already could tell,
But the pain I imparted on you has made it an impossibility,
And I know that.
But I cannot let you go, for now I know where my love lies.
I was tortured by my love for you, guilt filled my soul
endlessly because
I love you.

Yet on that day, the day in which it may have been our last
together,
We connected.
"Talia," "Theo," "Skye," and "Sean."
Our love immortalised within those names,
And how I wish them to be more than fantasy,
That is what they are.
Your soft touch, your eyes...perfect.
The eyes I want to wake next to every morning, the eyes I
cannot have.
I yearn to go back, fix what should never have been broken.
But that is impossible, isn't it?
My Christine may be lost and gone, I can still hear your
voice,
The perfect voice.
So fun and so talented, yet ever so humble.
I wish to see you one day, and when you perform, I shall be
there,
To see my Christine.

"My broken soul won't be alive and whole, 'til I hear you
sing, once more."

With Only a Note

With only a note, my life crumbled before me,
And the walls of joys ceased before my eyes.
What was once a love dissipated to ash in only six minutes.

Disappointed and angry, my fury increased like hellfire
within me,
A fury at myself, not those who caused it;
That's what happened after only a note.

Yet, with only a note, my companions disappeared before
me.
"Embarrassed and ashamed," is what they were,
But I do not blame them, for who would wish to be with
freaks.

Then, doors closed; infection soared through the polluted
air,
With warnings to "stay inside!", cemented my isolation to
be true.
An isolation caused with only a note.

In my turmoil, a note would never be heard from me,
Only tears and whimpers escaped my pained lungs.
The noises of harmony ended for what seemed like an
eternity;

The music of the night was over,

And I loathed as if I were a gargoyle forged in hell.

All a consequence of only a note.

But then, a support and glimmer of hope appeared,

An acceptance and a hand to lead me through the darkness

And into the light.

A belief reinstated in my soul,

And a guidance to allow me to soar,

An accomplishment which I will pursue.

For only a note made me reform,

And my future promises me to be reborn.

Red Mist

Why does this hot-flamed phoenix perch itself before my
eyes?
With its talons sinking itself deep into my forearm,
And its crimson iris staring intensely into my soul
And transferring its flame further into my heart.

I feel infused. It burns through my sternum like acid
And sinks its blade past my lungs and punctures the heart.
Yes, I know this flame is buried within me,
Yet it is not the flame of passion, but of pain.

My pure soul turned to temporary as this never-ending
Torture continues its mad work upon me.
Yet it's not just me who is affected.
The poor victims of my peril burn more than my molten
soul.

My lash and thrash towards their throats in snappy form,
Whilst not intentional, it still hurts as I were to sink my
talons into them.
With fiery venom seeping from my nails into their veins,
To share the rage red mist which surrounds me with them.

And when it simmers down and sizzles to ease, regret and
sorry discover me.

A quick apology to be handed out in prayer their veins are
not burning still.
This temporary disease is cruel and can scar,
Yet its inevitability to return is what burns the most.

The Man and The Great oak

I stare at the Great Oak and dream of it to stumble and
tumble
And fall down upon me,
Till I am no more than an imprint on the ground.

I will become one with the ground,
Allow the maggots and worms to feast
And grow their slimy wriggles to astronomical size,

And then I can live on through them.
Discard my physicality and face
And allow it to morph into another maggot.

Allow me to be the life for others,
Other creatures of the night,
Other disgusting and despised creatures.

Let the Great Oak fall and repeat the cycle,
Its slow cracks open the new door of life
To allow me to finish my story.

Death excites me at this moment,
That ardent curiosity to be fulfilled.
But I am too weak to let the Oak fall,

For I am not as Great as the Oak,

I'd simply let it crumble before my feet

And allow it to dodge my presence.

Who would want to be the reason for my death?

Who would waste that potential on me?

The Disappointment. The Disgust.

A Rhapsody of Life

Bb D, F, Bb, D, G, F
Bb Bb, G, F

Bb D, F, Bb, D, G, F
Bb Bb, G, F

My dearest Mother, he is now dead,
With a bang and a bullet throughout his brain and temple.
Oh Mother, I feel like I've just been born,
But what I have done will disintegrate all my hopes and
dreams.

It was never my intention to make your eyes flow their
rivers,
But if this is the last time you will see me as me,
Don't come looking for him.
Continue and live, as if I didn't exist.

Bb D, F, Bb, D, G, F
Bb Bb, G, F

Bb D, F, Bb, D, G, F
Bb Bb, G, F

My dearest mother, I am too far down the road,
I have passed the sign of my calling.
And though fear may crawl on my skin
And my chest burns with the agony of regret,

I have to say goodbye.
For my inevitability is that I must leave.
I need to shut the door on this life
And face what I've become.

Oh Mama!
I don't want to die!
I sometimes wish I'd never been born at all!

Heartburn

That familiar feeling of sickness boils in my bowels,
The tangy and fiery flame grows in my chest.
I eat what I enjoy, yet its repercussions act as my regret,
My body's regret, not my brain, for my brain is too
distracted to see.

I eat what I enjoy but look down and the enjoyment runs,
Fleeing like a hyena after its next goat.
As quick as it went in, I wish it would exit again,
So, I don't have to face that fiery guilt anymore.

I pray to grab the enthusiasm to change it,
Fix my addiction and find physical satisfaction.
But it's hard.
Hard to break away from what I enjoy.

I want to fix my problems, but I struggle.
I need to fix it, but it's hard.
I don't want to be this, but it is difficult to change.
I want to fix my struggles, but fixing may be the problem.

Still

Still, yet so ever present,
The only sound repeating is that of cars flying by.
But you sit so ever still, yet I feel you move,
For your cycle rolls round and round.
Never ending.

Your sister breezes past my cheeks, freezing them ever so,
Yet you stay still, and just let the wind blow.
Not a sound of crash nor whoosh comes from you,
For you sit so still.
So ever still.

In your stillness there is beauty,
A calming and relaxing presence generated by no other.
Your being brings true peace, an assistance.
One which to help me bury inner turmoil,
For you bring peace.

That silence you so sweetly supplied now shatters.
Crashing against the rock in your threatening ways,
For when I stand before you face to face,
And your peace threatens me to tread lightly.
For your eternal peace you do not want us to tarnish.

Her power and glory bestowed upon you,
To be respected as you have done eternally.

Yet in her world is torment and suffering,
And you must exist and watch.
You must exist and watch.

Tomorrow is a New Day

The fireball of hope ceases as it returns to its rest,
And its replacement is nothing more than darkness and death,
Death of the day gone by.
It does not matter to me; tomorrow is a new day.

Yet in this darkness I see despair rush through,
Only a glimmer of hope peeking out from behind the barriers.
Yet that's all it is, a peek. The darkness killed and consumed the hope it gave.
There is nothing for me here, nothing for me now.

The love of nature I saw in those gorgeous greens
Are now caped in darkness, no more life to be squeezed from them.
I see myself in these forms of nature: day filled with love and life,
Yet night filled with death and suffering.

What is there for me?
When the day is done, am I nothing but a pawn in God's plan to entertain?
I provide and I give. Yet what am I to the world?
A distraction to the horror surrounding us? From the murder and horridness of life?

I will never know, but I'm satisfied with that.

My life is good, well health, and help to distract me from my pains.

My toils and heartache are covered by the Gift,

The Gift we all have, yet it is in different wrapping for you and me.

Question Marks

It was in that moment I knew,
I knew that you were all I ever needed.
After all the years searching for someone new,
It was your love I looked to God and pleaded.

To be joined as one with a vow and a kiss,
It is a dream of mine which I pray to be real.
To love our own family is a chance I cannot miss,
With looks of love and smiles at our family meals.

Yet that dream creeps away as you fly to your future,
And my heart will be shattered without your presence.
Shattered like glass as I miss your glow and your humor,
And I will cry sleepless nights yearning for your grace and
benevolence.

You have filled my life with so many question marks,
Yet it is with you my real life will start.

The Moment

In time we discover what we are, as we dig our shovel of
curiosity deep within,
Which was previously buried in questions and queries we
could not yet comprehend.
"Truth lies within," I once heard, and only now may I
understand.

Yet, as we penetrate the layer of protection,
We see the true horror which inherits our soul. Forever in
purgatory. Forever in fear.
Fear of what the future beholds, yet we are enticed with
knowledge as we pursue inward.

And as we enter the void of truth, we see nothing but air.
But a light! Like an outstretched hand beckoning us
forward!
We cannot turn back; we're past the point of No Return.

It leads us down a dark tunnel, with random lights flashing
before us,
Innocent memories circle our vision, and I chuckle and
point with a smile.
Yet, as I focus back on the truth, a sigh involuntarily
escapes me, a cry for the past long lost.

Now, we are at the epicentre of life. We have finally learnt
all we need to know!
But I ask myself... why? Why could I not remain curious?
Why could I not question?
A tear falls down my cheek, and I beg for forgiveness.

My prayer is not answered. As Adam betrayed God, God
too has betrayed me.
And I am condemned to an eternal Hell. This is no Eden,
For that is fiction. Pandemonium is the truth. I am chained
in an eternal Hell!

I turn my back upon thee. I have discovered the truth.
I have discovered The Moment.
You no longer reign upon my world; I shall tread upon my
path in familiar soil.

My shovel of curiosity has discovered more than dirt and
rocks,
I have discovered the truth in my life. I am the eternal king
upon my very existence.
You can no longer chain my limbs with your power; I shall
destroy all barriers you lay down.

I shall look upon my future not in fear, yet in hope,
For I am free from my cage.
This is my moment.

Parallel Paths

When I need you, your hand will be there to reach for me,
And when I ask for your guidance, you will give me your
eyes,
And if I want your love, it has been granted before I called.
But all of this comes to my lack of care.
My love for you will be eternal,
So, I can relish in your grace,
But my attention is diverted,
And my eyes are adopted elsewhere.
Profession, romance, future—
Whatever it may be. It has led me astray.
I have walked to the right of the parallel paths,
Only looking left when I am selfish enough to look.
But when I look across that way, I yearn to walk back.
A need to return to the path which I was set on at birth.
A need to step onto the good soil and not to be choked by
thorns.
But a need I have been distracted from.

And when I am fulfilled, I will walk back.
Step my foot onto the left path and start my journey.

Inevitable

A morning of Maybe.
A morning of Chance.
A moment in time to discover how I end my story,
How I may call the curtain on a seven-year play.

Staring into that golden break between the clouds,
My ears surrounded by Schoenberg and Boubil,
And my eyes attracted to the sun of future.
For in one hour, I shall discover the closing sentence to my
novel.

And as I step through those pearly black gates
That I have stepped through thousands of times.
Maybe this will be the step that mattered,
Or maybe it will not.

For this is a chance,
A maybe,
A discovery.
We will see how the gods write my scripture.

//

Yet it is not to be.
The curtain fell early.
And I am left in the dark of disappointment.

What if I did more?
What if I did better?
But I know I did all I could,
Nothing more for me to do.
It was simply inevitable.

Journey Toward the End

Maybe this journey will be the last,

The last train to unity,

The last step on this stage.

Or at least the last time with all of you.

The last time squeezed together chair by chair

And our voices blended to four...or more,

The last time to perform under the watchful eye of you,

And whilst I know your support will continue for me,

My time with you comes to an end.

My chapter is finished,

And my saga has closed its cover for one last time.

Or at least, closed its cover with you.

No more laughs

And no more moments.

However, I will reflect and wish for more,

One more moment.

But that would be selfish, wouldn't it?

We do not all get our fairytale send-off

Despite how much I thought I did to achieve it.

No.

My swan song will remain sombre,

And nor is it my swan song.

But that is that and this is this.

The journey and pleasure have been all mine,

Yet the fates allow this end not to be for me.

I am simply the cameo to this scenery,
Like a shadow to your figure.
But that is that and this is this,
Just a journey toward the end.

Fantasy

My dearest loving wife, or so I wish to call you,
So caring and gentle, yet not mine to be true.
My love for you beams and radiates; I could shout it all night!
But I sit with a painful smile. I watch you love another: a murderous sight.

We talk and we joke, we laugh and we live,
But my love remains unspoken, and our marriage a myth.
The endless nights loom on in despair and in prayer,
Not just for your happiness, but for our love to be true.

"Right person. Wrong time." that's what I tell myself,
For a glimmer of hope to remain, of what could be.
I will love you unconditionally and thank God for your appearance.
If we were one, my life would be complete in a moment.

My dearest loving wife, I love you for life.
But your love for another, not mine, never.
The one who gave me the world but never saw it leave their hands,
The one who showed me true human beauty,

The one who showed me love I didn't deserve,
The love I will never find.

No one can love me till I love myself,

And I shall never love myself till someone loves me.

Chain Pillow
For Pussy Boots

Dearest chain pillow, without you what would I be?
Perhaps a loner or in sadness, but that could never be.
For the fun you give that short break time
Reminds me of years spent with you, the years gone by and
by.

The rush of adrenaline which you inject into my veins
Resembles the excitement I feel from friends that will
always reign.
The hits and whacks of softness against my face
Make me cry with laughter, which fills the whole place.

A group of outcasts united in our strange ways,
Blending perfectly together, no matter how weird they may
say.
They'd give us looks. Tell us to grow up.
But we know they are jealous that they'd never have our
luck.

The chain pillow resembles us, as do many other things,
No matter how strange, we love the joy it brings.
I would never change this group, never trade for another.
We are meant to be together, the brothers from other
mothers.

Amen

I, who may appear as a prophet or scholar to those ahead,
Sit in comfort stalking over their pressure and fears.
As they stare at the questions of future to be answered in
paper and pen,
And tremble as they do so, whilst they glance up in jealousy
toward a prophet.

Yet I am not a prophet; they are truly mistaken.
Not even a decade has passed since I was one of them,
Not even a decade has passed since I trembled and glanced
at prophets.
But they do not know that I sit in pressure and fear, with my
future stalking over me.

They likely think I gaze with pure sympathy; how I wish that
were the case!
I sit in empathy. How I yearn to go back to those golden
childhood days.
The days which spoke of care and permanent joy... gone.
Now, a future looming of promise, a future looming of pain.

Next year a new group will roll in, and I will be gone.
Doing what I love most, and they will work on.
This viscous cycle of education will live for years to come,
And when sharing my art to the world, I won't forget where
I came from.

Yet this day is not for me, I am but a pawn.

What's important is they're blessed and guided to glory.

My own path is one I must accomplish alone,

For my work and determination is my key. My future.

Bless them all with your love and grace,

Your strength and power,

Your patience and knowledge.

Bless them *all* with your love and grace.

Camino

Each step I take is a step of Hell upon Earth,
With every footprint remaining in the clay crying painful
tears.
A step of torture, yet one to discover my human worth,
A step out of purgatory, a step out of fears.

Heavily geared for the treacherous journey lying before my
feet,
Yet I am prepared; my physical pain is subsided for pride
and joy.
For if successful, which my persistence must allow me to
meet,
I shall meet you there, and I will arrive as a man, not a boy.

For I know I have done what I have come here to do.
Your name, your legacy to be immortalised on a carved
stone,
And I complete this journey for my life, and for you.
I must do it, I must. For all the love you have shown.

And as you fly toward his kingdom, on a heavenly dove,
I allow your legacy to live on in this earth, in my heart, and
in love.

What Goes on Below

We never really know what goes on below,

And you, my friend, are no exception.

I saw you every day and thought it was all figured out,

Your beaming smile, surrounded by those who are friends;

You were simply admirable.

Then she came along, and upon the surface it appeared as if

you were Romeo.

Oh! What if I really knew!

Yet I could not know; your beam would not drop.

Never a slouch. Never an issue.

How could anyone know what really went on below?

Then I saw what you had to say; the heart was speaking,

not the mask.

Your words struck sympathy in my heart not yet conceived

by another,

And now I look upon you with sadness; you are not a

slouch, but a survivor.

And I apologise for not being there in your time of need. I

ignored your cry,

And I nearly lost you there, our connections to be broken.

"The connection will always be present,"

You taught me so much without realizing,

You trusted me and shared your love in writing.

I promise I will be better, and I will love whatever it is you

show,

For I now know what is really going on below.

Expression

You ask me to express in ways that are familiar to you,
But I cannot be the person you want.
I cannot adapt myself to fit your need,
Nor will I let myself become what I am not,
Despite how hard it may be for me,
Despite how much I feel forever trapped.

I can't be real! I cannot be me.
Free from my chains? An impossible want.
Held down, barred from freedom. Forever trapped.
Trapped by those who thought they would help. Trapped by
you.
I feel like with you around I must be what I am not,
Never what I want, only what you need.

Must I be the dog muzzled and trapped?
Or am I but a marionette to be controlled for what they
need?
Or am I human? Who can live and think as I want?
No—that is impossible. After all, that's not the want of
you.
I must follow orders and salute to you, for who cares for
me?
What I have to say. Is it important? It is not.

Who am I? Who is me?

Can I be whatever I want?
Whatever I need?
Should I still love you despite what you say makes me
think you do not?
Or should I be a good boy and follow the needs of you?
Even though I will be trapped in my mind, and in my
body... trapped.

That's why I do what I want
Alone. So you can't judge me for being me,
And what is in writing is what only I need.
Contained and alone, what I feel must be trapped
Away from the devils and demons such as you.
Only to be seen by those who understand, for you do not.

But I continue to dream of showing you me,
For you to be proud of every part of me as I am to you.
If you were able to listen to me, to listen to the speech I
want,
Then maybe I won't feel so trapped.
You'd give me your ear to listen when I need,
Like you once did.

If you do this, I won't feel so trapped.
The words I want to say will be the words of me,
I'll speak the words which I need. *Never* the ones I do not.

No Matter What

As far as I must travel, as far as I must walk,

Not a single step will be felt of my feet touching the
ground,

Not a single penny will be noticed fleeing the jail of my
bank,

For it does not have any relevance for me,

Because my love for you has no boundaries,

No end in sight,

No spike to pop my tires,

No man to hold me back—nothing—

For my love has no boundaries when my love is with you,

And I lose a part of myself when I am not next to you,

When you are not in my arms,

And your sweet scent makes me succumb to your hypnosis,

And I simply just allow it.

I will allow it only if it is your hypnosis.

I have written my novel with you as the protagonist.

I've casted my play with you in the leading role.

My novel is called

You.

My play is called

You.

My life is called

You.

Addiction

Line by line and hit by hit
Comes that sense of guilt which is inevitable to follow.
The pleasure is always followed by pain,
The thought of "why?"
Before I return to do it again soon after.

Do I need to? No.
Do I want to? Sometimes.
But I hate that feeling after,
That feeling of why and what which made me do it.
The addiction will continue its cycle, line by line.

I am not alone in my addiction.
And I believe it is just for now,
And it will stop soon—I hope.
I pray. For my shame will grow and grow
Until my shame has climaxed.

Under the Influence

My eyes daze and my eyes fumble
With my head swaying side to side
Unintentionally.
And all is a blur ahead, a haze of what once was,
A carpet of grey reflecting like a pool.
Boys and girls laugh and joke beside me,
But in the corner sits a lonely man.
He is physically
And mentally
Alone.
This toxic poison tucks my brain into the bed of sedation,
And allows me to feel calmness over my soul
And to breathe again,
Without the weight of the world pulling me down.

And all these thoughts are because of that toxic poison,
Disguised in fizz and pop,
But what rests at the bottom is a demon.
The Devil in liquid form:
I say things I don't want to say,
And do things I don't want to do,
All because of you.

May I return home with lipstick smeared across my lips,
Kissing the wrong girl, but just to kiss.
Or do I return with sick in my stomach,

Knowing the mistakes I have injected
Into my deteriorating stomach.

An addiction,
A hate,
A love.

I hate I need this to feel free,
But I love this feeling when gaining the key.

Floof

You are still in my life, why do I cry like a child?
You are still living, so why do I miss you already?
In your prime, some would say, so lively and loving,
So why do I mourn you yet?

The minuscule thought of it brings me to weeping wails.
Your certain spots on the sofas,
The hairs you leave behind with every step you take,
And your annoying yet amazing barks which surround the
streets.

So, why do I weep?
Is it because of the inevitable loss of your golden haze in the
corner?
Or is it your jolts and jumps up and down the landing?
Is it your presence? An aura no other pup could replace.

Your golden glow and stinky breath,
Bark-brown eyes and bushy white tail,
A simple pitter-patter on the second floor,
And the dinosaur which is released when tickling that bit too
hard.

That burst of excitement when a familiar person steps in,
An inspirational energy I wish I could adopt into my life.

But when that jolt of lightning in your veins dims down,

That's when I will know your time has come.

I think I weep for the thought of watching you leave.

Those bark-brown eyes close that one last time,

That bushy white tail stops wagging,

And to return home without a pitter-patter to be heard.

Confliction and Confusion

I am for you, and you are for me. I knew that and wanted that,

And I think I still do? But not as sure as I was before.

My confusion grows each time we are together,

For you say we are platonic, yet I only see romantic.

But I still convince myself that it is what you say,

Despite how much I feel for you.

Or that was the case until another door was opened,

Painted bright yellow and with a welcoming entrance,

And it averts my gaze to focus on its attractive colours.

But as I walk towards it my heart rips out from my back

And stays in that central state of confliction and confusion,

For it knows my real feelings, that which I am still unsure of.

Why can't I leave her?

Where would I start?

But maybe I need to abandon my heart so I can find a new one,

Despite how much I will look back toward the old one.

But what if I find my new heart and it doesn't fit me?

Would I return to the old?

Or would I search again?

The question I do not have the answer to.

Confusion and confliction are what I feel right now,

But somehow when I am with you it disappears.

My mind is clear. And I am home.

I Will Always Love You

It was that one night when I knew I had lost you,

Despite never losing anything.

But it felt like it.

Like the heart was ripped out of my chest

And crushed before my eyes.

Heartbreak.

That's what your words felt like when you told me.

We were never one. Yet I held out hope.

We would never be one. Yet I held out hope.

You love me, but not the same. Never.

We would be married, I thought, no matter how long it took,

And I'd still wait for you, even if your heart lies

Elsewhere.

Not for me to hold

Nor for me to kiss.

Your embrace for him,

And your lips for him.

You hold my heart in the palm of your hands,

unknowingly.

And there it will stay,

For life

And forever.

A note.

I didn't have a title for this poem when I wrote it, and after thinking for a while I couldn't conclude what I wanted to call this poem. I was trying to make it relevant to the content written, but that's not what is important.

If the title doesn't tell the truth, then the content is pointless, and the poem is pointless.

I love you. I will always love you, No matter how far. No matter who I meet. It means nothing.

You are my world, my rock, my all.

Crater in the Clouds

With power and thrust, we burst up and up,
Us all equal in the palm of this metal hand,
Safely stuck and passionately held when we fly and soar,
Knowing when we arrive, we arrive in joyful hope.
Yet as we fly, we hover in a perpendicular line, not
changing nor altering,
Yet as we fly, we travel to the same place for our different
motives.
Me—I fly to find home, where I find love and appreciation,
Where I can set the next chapter in the novel I am
authoring.
Buckled and rested on this metal bird, with soothing sounds
Of Boe surrounding my ears, such sweet vibrato to bring
me home.
Gazing out the minuscule window at pink glow and amber
light radiating
Through the panes, and sensually embracing my eyes with
its beauty,
As it has done many times in many forms before.
Through this pink glow is this dark hole... a dark hole?
This spiralling crater in the clouds wearing a light and
fluffy hat,
Yet a disgusting dark body the deeper you look.
Why in such a beautiful image is there a sinister undertone?
Could it possibly be telling me of the storm to come?

Or could it be warning me of a mistake which I'd make on my journey?

With its circular form hypnotising my eyes to its attraction,

Nature has again succeeded in holding me in the palm of its hand.

My eyes are made fool to this sensation, with no one else noticing it,

As if this crater chose me to deceive, to try distract me from my objective.

My will is stronger than that; not even nature could distract me.

I would not allow it.

This crater falls into memory as I soar on by, with power and thrust.

My goal falls to bring him home and epic love and pop songs.

To defy the symbolic evil that dark menace presented, to prove my will

Is stronger than that of deceit, that I am the one to decide when

I back down. But I will not back down, and I will not fall.

I fly toward my future, and I will prove I am worthy of this future.

As everyone has their future planned in his eyes,

He has planned this for me,

And I will be the one to achieve it.

Ascending
For Hugo Reilly-Stewart

If I could freeze time, I would, so I could stay here.
With the breeze pressing against my face, gently.
With the sounds of strings cancelling out the growls of the
cars running behind me.
With peace finally returning to me, in this tranquil place.
With bright lights illuminating the night sky, not a cloud in
sight.
With the ocean so still across the bed, not a gust could
move it.
The smoothness of my seat creating the perfect mattress for
my rest.
And again, the sound of strings cancelling out my fears.
So light,
And so delicate.
That angelic sound will resonate with me for life,
That sound a friend introduced me to.
But so much more than a friend he was,
For he was an inspiration,
A talent:
So light,
And so delicate.
A relationship with a bow stronger than any love possible,
Admirable.
When you ascended the lark, you ascended me.
And when I hear that delicate bow kiss the string,

You will be in my mind.

With the world so still at my feet,

I could die here now,

If you were the one who said goodbye to me.

Through your music,

Through your song,

Through your love.

Flowing Thoughts is based on the experiences of the poet, Jack Cairns, throughout 2023-2024. However, this collection isn't meant just for him; it's interpretable and insightful for all teenagers, all adults, all humans.

You can relate to many, if not all, poems within this collection, adapting them to your own life or experiences. That was his intention. Teenage life is hard, and sometimes we believe no one else will understand. But if you're struggling with anything during this tough time, you're not alone.

It is okay to not be okay.

-Cairnsy